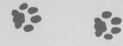

a DOG waLKS

INTO a Bar...

DOG JOKES SO FUNNY
YOU'LL BEG FOR MORE

Illustrations *by* Tim McGee

LARK BOOKS

A Division of Sterling Publishing Co., Inc
New York / London

Development Editor: Deborah Morgenthal
Editor: Joanne O'Sullivan
Art Direction: Herter Studio LLC, San Francisco, CA
Interior and cover design: Debbie Berne
Illustrator: Tim McGee

Library of Congress Cataloging-in-
Publication Data

A dog walks into a bar : dog jokes so
funny you'll beg for more / edited by
Joanne O'Sullivan. — 1st ed.
    p. cm.
  ISBN-13: 978-1-60059-154-9
  (pb-trade pbk. : alk. paper)
  ISBN-10: 1-60059-154-X
  (pb-trade pbk. : alk. paper)
  1. Dogs—Humor. I. O'Sullivan,
Joanne
  PN6231.D68D63 2007
  818'.602—dc22
                    2007007795

10 9 8 7 6 5 4 3 2 1

First Edition

Published by Lark Books, A Division
of Sterling Publishing Co., Inc.
387 Park Avenue South,
New York, N.Y. 10016

Text © 2007, Lark Books
Illustrations © 2007, Tim McGee

Distributed in Canada by
Sterling Publishing,
c/o Canadian Manda Group,
165 Dufferin Street
Toronto, Ontario, Canada M6K 3H6

Distributed in the United Kingdom by
GMC Distribution Services,
Castle Place, 166 High Street, Lewes,
East Sussex, England BN7 1XU

Distributed in Australia by Capricorn
Link (Australia) Pty Ltd.,
P.O. Box 704, Windsor, NSW 2756
Australia

If you have questions or comments
about this book, please contact:
Lark Books
67 Broadway
Asheville, NC 28801
(828) 253-0467

Manufactured in China

ISBN 13: 978-1-60059-154-9
ISBN 10: 1-60059-154-X

For information about custom edi-
tions, special sales, premium and
corporate purchases, please contact
Sterling Special Sales Department
at 800-805-5489 or specialsales@
sterlingpub.com.

A CAT AND A DOG WALK INTO A BAR TOGETHER, snuggling and licking each other's fur.

"What is this?" the bartender asks.

"Some kind of a joke?"

🐾 CONTENTS

TRUE TO THEIR REPUTATION, dogs really are loyal, devoted, and dependable. But that's not why we love them. We love them because they make us laugh. The way they sleep in the laundry basket or happily shake their soaking wet fur all over anyone who happens to be standing nearby—it may look like instinctive animal behavior, but dog lovers know they're doing it for a bit of fun. Dogs amuse themselves while keeping us amused—maybe that's why they're our best friends.

This collection is full of jokes that both you and your dog can laugh at. Fetch a dog-hair covered chair, flip the pages, and enjoy. Or read the book aloud to your precious pooch (skip over any parts that might be offensive to his or her breed). Chances are you'll both be howling in minutes. From one-liners to shaggy dog stories, you're bound to discover jokes that will tickle your funny bone—if your dog hasn't already taken it and buried it in the backyard.

CHAPTER 1

A DOG WALKS INTO A BAR

Dogs get thirsty. And sometimes toilet bowl water just won't do.

A DOG WALKS INTO A BAR,

jumps onto a barstool, and says to the bartender,

"Hey, today is my birthday.

Do I get a free drink?"

The bartender replies,

"Sure, the toilet is around the corner."

Q. WHAT DO YOU CALL A GATHERING OF POMERANIANS AT A BAR? ··············

A DOG WALKS INTO A BAR,
A second dog walks into a bar.
The third one ducks.

A DOG WALKS INTO A BAR,

"How are you doing?" asks the bartender.
"Ruff," the dog answers.

Q. What's a dog's favorite wine?
A. "Please, please, please throw my ball!"

A BULLDOG WALKS INTO A BAR.

"Hey," says the bartender, "we have a cocktail named after you!"

"What . . . Bruiser?" asks the Bulldog.

A GUY WALKS INTO A BAR WITH A DOG. The bartender tells him dogs aren't allowed in the bar.

"But," the guy says, "my dog is really amazing. He speaks, understands every word I say, and follows my command."

"Prove it," says the bartender.

"OK, I'll get him to fetch the paper."

"Well, a lot of dogs can do *that*," the bartender says.

"And pay for it, and return the change?" the man asks.

"OK, this I've got to see," says the bartender.

The man hands the dog a hundred dollar bill, and tells the dog to go get him a paper.

"I'm on my way," says the dog, and he takes off.

"Don't forget my change!" the man yells after the dog.

One hour goes by, and the dog hasn't returned.

Two hours go by, and still no dog.

Three hours go by, and the owner is starting to get worried, so he goes out to look for the dog.

As he's walking down the street, he sees the dog walking toward him, decked out in a fancy dog sweater and wearing a rhinestone-encrusted collar, carrying a package of chew toys in his mouth.

"Fido! How could you? You've never done this before! Why now?"

The dog puts down the package. "Well, boss," he says, "I never had a hundred bucks before."

A GREAT DANE WALKS INTO A BAR and calls to the bartender, "I'll have a Scotch and . . . . water."

The bartender looks at the Dane and says, "What's with the long pause?"

"These?" he asks, looking down at his feet,

"I've had them all my life."

Q. WHAT DO YOU CALL A DOG WHO DRINKS TOO MUCH? ·······················

A DOG WALKS INTO A BAR. "Can I have a bottle of Heineken and a packet of pretzels, please?"

"Sure," says the bartender. He hands over the beer and pretzels and the dog takes a seat over in a booth.

A man sitting down at the bar watches the scene in amazement. After the dog leaves, he turns to the guy next to him and says, "Did you see that? That dog just ordered a beer and pretzels!"

"So?" the man nonchalantly asks, returning to his drink.

"Well, don't you think that's a bit unusual?" the first man asks.

"Well, now that you mention it, I guess it is," says the second guy. "He usually orders chips."

A DOG WALKS INTO A BAR AND ORDERS A BEER. The bartender gives it to him and says, "That'll be five dollars."

A little later, making conversation, the bartender says, "We don't get many dogs in here."

The dog replies, "At these prices . . . I'm not surprised."

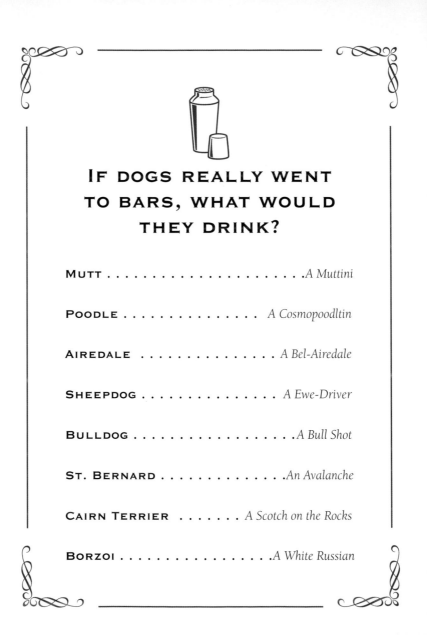

IF DOGS REALLY WENT TO BARS, WHAT WOULD THEY DRINK?

MUTT . . . . *A Muttini*

POODLE . . . . *A Cosmopoodltin*

AIREDALE . . . . *A Bel-Airedale*

SHEEPDOG . . . . *A Ewe-Driver*

BULLDOG . . . . *A Bull Shot*

ST. BERNARD . . . . *An Avalanche*

CAIRN TERRIER . . . . *A Scotch on the Rocks*

BORZOI . . . . *A White Russian*

A DOG WALKS INTO A BAR, walks up to the bartender, and asks, "Have you got any dog food?"

The bartender says, "No."

The dog asks again, "Have you got any dog food?"

"No," says the bartender, getting irritated.

"Have you got any dog food?" the dog asks again, unfazed.

"No! I don't," says the bartender, losing his temper, "and if you ask me one more time I'm gonna nail you to the wall by your ears!"

The dog pauses for a moment.

"Have you got any nails?" he asks.

"No," says the bartender, suspiciously.

"Have you got any dog food?" the dog asks.

CHAPTER 2
WONDERDOGS AND UNDERDOGS

Dog geniuses. And some not so much.

THREE FRIENDS ARE BRAGGING ABOUT THEIR DOGS: each claims to have the world's smartest.

"My dog is so smart," the first friend says, "every morning I give him a five dollar bill and he goes to Starbucks and buys me a latte. He even comes back with the correct change. Now that's a smart dog."

"That's nothing," the second friend says. "My dog goes to Starbucks every morning and picks up a mocha *and* a newspaper for me. Now *that's* a smart dog."

The third friend shakes his head and grins. "You know the Starbucks where your dogs go every morning? My dog's the manager there."

A DOG WEARING A TOOL BELT walks into a busy diner and sits down at the counter. He orders the blue plate special.

"Oh my gosh," says the waitress. "You can talk!"

"Your ears work well," says the dog.

"But you're a dog," she replies.

"Nothing wrong with your eyes either," the dog says.

"Well, what brings you in here?" she asks, seeming to get used to the idea of a talking dog.

"I'm working at the building site across the street for a few weeks," he says. "I'll probably see you a lot at lunch time."

Each day he comes in and orders lunch.

One day, the circus comes to town. The ringmaster comes to the diner for breakfast and the waitress tells him about the talking dog. "You should get him for your circus," she says. "People would pay a lot of money to see a talking dog. I'll ask him for you."

When the dog comes in at lunch, she says, "I was talking to the circus ringmaster this morning. He's interested in hiring you. You could make a lot of money there."

"At the circus?" the dog asks, looking perplexed. "What do they want with a construction worker?"

A SALESMAN went to visit one of his clients. He walked in to find the office empty except for a dog. The man watched in amazement as the dog, dressed in an apron, vacuumed the room and emptied the wastebaskets. The dog looked up, saw the man watching him, and said, "Don't mind me. This is all part of my job."

The man looked at the dog in amazement and said, "Wow, a talking dog! Does your boss know about this?"

"Please don't tell him!" the dog begged. "If he finds out about this he'll have me answering the phones as well!"

A GERMAN SHEPHERD walks into a telegram office. He takes a blank form and writes:

"Woof. Woof. Woof. Woof. Woof. Woof. Woof. Woof. Woof."

The clerk examines the form and politely tells him: "There are only nine words here. You could send another Woof for the same price."

The dog looks at her as if she's a bit dim. "Yeah," he says, "but that wouldn't make any sense."

A MAN WENT TO VISIT A FRIEND and was amazed to find him playing chess with his dog.

"I can hardly believe my eyes!" he exclaimed. "That's the smartest dog I've ever seen."

"Oh, he's not so smart," the friend replied. "I've beaten him three games out of five."

AN EVANGELICAL COUPLE was looking for a dog, so they went to a kennel specializing in Christian pets. They found one that they liked a lot and took him home.

To test his faith, they asked him to fetch the Bible, and he did it with ease. When they instructed him to look up Psalm 23, he found it without a problem.

That night, they had friends over. They were so proud of their new dog that they decided to show off a little. "Our dog is full of the spirit of the Lord," they said. "We believe he could even work miracles."

"Well," said the friends, "we'd like to see that."

The husband thought about it for a moment. "Bob," he said to his friend, "are you still having those headaches?"

"Yes," said the friend. "Terrible migraines."

The man whispered in his dog's ear, and the dog nodded as if in understanding. He went to the friend, closed his eyes, and placed his paw on the man's forehead.

"**Heal!**" the man commanded.

A MAN WALKS INTO A BAR with a small dog under his arm. The bartender says, "Sorry, pal. No dogs allowed."

"But this is a special dog," the man says. "He talks!"

"Yeah, right," says the bartender. "Now get out of here before I throw you out."

"No, wait," pleads the man. "I'll prove it." He turns to the dog and asks, "What do you normally find on top of a house?"

"Roof!" says the dog, wagging his tail.

"Give me a break . . . " says the bartender.

"Wait," says the man, "I'll ask another question." He turns to the dog again and asks, "What's the opposite of soft?"

"Ruff!" exclaims the dog.

"Quit wasting my time," says the bartender.

"One more chance," pleads the man. Turning to the dog again, he asks, "Who was the greatest baseball player that ever lived?"

"Ruth!" barks the dog.

"Okay, that's it!" yells the bartender, and he throws them both out into the street.

The dog turns to his owner and shrugs, "Maybe I should have said DiMaggio?"

A WOMAN LOOKING FOR A DOG sees an ad in the local paper. "Pedigree Labrador For Sale: Only 100 dollars."

When she arrives at the owner's house, he shows her into the living room where the Labrador is relaxing in front of the fire.

"Well, what kind of pedigree does the dog have?" she inquires.

"Why not ask him yourself?" says the owner.

Surprised and skeptical, she asks the dog, "Well hey there, fella, what is your pedigree?"

"My mother was a three-time Best in Show winner at the Westminster Dog Show and my father was a runner-up," replies the dog. "I was trained by the CIA at Quantico and spent several years doing undercover work in Latin America. After that, I headed the Department of Homeland Security's bomb-sniffing operation for a few years."

Astonished, the woman asks, "Why on earth would you want to sell this dog?"

"Because he's such a liar!" says the owner.

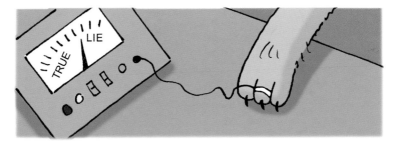

A LARGE DOG walks into a butcher shop, carrying a purse in his mouth. He puts the purse down and sits in front of the meat case.

"What is it, boy?" the butcher jokingly asks. "Want to buy some meat?"

"Woof!" barks the dog.

"What kind?" asks the butcher. "Liver, bacon, steak ..."

"Woof!" interrupts the dog.

"And how much steak? Half a pound, one pound ..."

"Woof!" signals the dog.

The amazed butcher wraps up the meat and finds the money in the dog's purse. As the dog leaves, the butcher decides to follow him. The dog enters an apartment building, climbs to the top floor, and begins scratching at a door. With that, the door swings open and the owner starts reprimanding him.

"How can you yell at him!" the butcher exclaims. "He's the most intelligent animal I've ever seen!"

"Intelligent?" the owner replies. "This is the third time this week he's forgotten his key!"

CHAPTER 3
MAN'S BEST FRIEND, CAT'S WORST ENEMY

The funny side of the war between the species

THE DIFFERENCE BETWEEN DOGS AND CATS

DOGS come when you call them.
CATS take a message and get back to you.

DOGS will bark to wake you up if the house is on fire.
CATS will quietly sneak out the back door.

DOGS will bring you your slippers or the evening newspaper.
CATS might bring you a dead mouse.

DOGS will play Frisbee with you all afternoon.
CATS will take a three-hour nap.

DOGS will greet you and lick your face when you come home from work.
CATS will be mad that you went to work at all.

DOGS will sit, lie down, and heel on command. **CATS** will smirk and walk away.

DOGS will tilt their heads and listen whenever you talk. **CATS** will yawn and close their eyes.

DOGS will give you unconditional love forever. **CATS** will make you pay for every mistake you've ever made.

A DOG IN A FOOTBALL JERSEY is walking down the street when he sees a building on fire. A lady is standing on a third-story ledge, holding her cat in her arms.

"Hey, lady," says the dog, "throw me the cat."

"No way," she shouts back through the flames.

"I'm a wide receiver with the Dallas Cowboys," he says. "I can catch him."

A crowd gathers around to witness the scene. "It's true!" says one of the passersby. "He's that famous football-playing dog!"

"Come on, lady, hurry. If you do it now, I can save your cat," the dog calls out again.

"Why should I trust you?" she shouts back. "You're a dog!"

"It's now or never," the dog shouts back. "I'm a great re-ceiver. I know I can catch him."

Seeing the flames move closer, the woman kisses her cat and tosses him down.

The dog runs toward it, keeping his eyes on it the whole time. He jumps six feet into the air and makes a spectacular one-handed catch. The crowd breaks into cheers.

The dog gets up on his hind legs, does a little dance, lifts the cat above his head, wiggles his knees back and forth, then spikes the cat.

A MAN LET HIS DOG OUT in the backyard one night, then went back inside to have dinner and watch a little TV. After a few hours, he remembered that he hadn't let the dog back in yet, so he went to the back door and called him.

He was horrified when the dog came back with the neighbor's cat in his mouth, dead as a doornail. "Bad dog! Bad dog!" he said.

Panicked, he picked up the cat and took it into the kitchen. He looked over at his neighbor's darkened house and remembered that they had been away for the weekend and would be back later that night. He had to come up with a plan.

He took the cat into the bathroom, washed and scrubbed the dirt off it and blow-dried its fur. Then he snuck over and placed the cat on the neighbor's front porch and dashed back home. He hoped the neighbor would think the cat had died of a heart attack.

The next morning, his neighbor knocked on the door. The man answered with his heart pounding, sweat starting to form on his brow.

"I guess you heard what happened," the neighbor said.

"No," said the man, with a crack in his voice. "What is it?"

"We had a death in our family," the neighbor replied.

"I'm sorry," said the man. "Who died?"

"Fluffy," said the neighbor. "But the weird thing is that after we buried him, someone dug him up, cleaned him off, and put him on the front porch."

A DOG DIES OF NATURAL CAUSES and goes to heaven. When he meets God, God says, "You've been a good dog and you've lived a good life. What do you want as your reward?"

The dog thinks for a moment.

"I lived my whole life with a poor family," he says. "I never had a dog bed. I think that would be my idea of heaven."

"Of course," says God, and a dog bed appears.

A few days later, six cats are killed in a tragic accident and go to heaven.

God greets them and makes them the same offer.

"All of our lives we have been chased by dogs," one says. "We are tired of running. Could we have some roller skates?"

"Certainly," says God, and the roller skates appear.

About a week later, God stops by to see how the dog is doing.

God finds him lying comfortably in the dog bed.

"How are things since you arrived?" God asks.

The dog stretches and sighs with contentment. "Heaven is great," he says. "Better than I could ever have expected. I just love those meals on wheels you keep sending over."

A MAN TOOK HIS DOG TO THE VET. The vet examined the dog, took his temperature, felt his abdomen, and looked in his mouth. When he was done, he shook his head.

"I'm sorry," he said. "Your dog has kidney failure. He has two days left to live."

The man was devastated and demanded a second opinion.

"Well, all right," said the vet. He picked up the phone and muttered something the man couldn't hear.

A few minutes later, a cat came walking into the room and quickly looked the dog over. She turned to the vet and said, "Kidney failure."

"That's what I thought," said the vet.

"You must be joking," said the man, becoming irate. "I'm not taking a cat's opinion. Get someone else."

"Very well," said the vet, picking up the phone again. Once again, he muttered a few words and hung up.

A few minutes later, a Labrador walked in. He examined the dog briefly, then said, "Kidney failure."

"My thoughts exactly," said the vet.

"This is absurd," said the man. "I'm leaving."

"That will be 300 dollars," said the vet.

"You've got to be kidding," said the man. "Three hundred dollars for that?"

"It wasn't just my services," said the vet. "You also had the cat scan and the Lab report."

CHAPTER 4

GOOD BREEDING

These days, anything goes.

Q. WHY ARE GERMAN BOXERS SUCH A RARE BREED? ·····························

A YOUNG SOCIAL CLIMBER went to her local kennel to look for a pet.

"I want only the highest quality dog," she told the saleswoman. "Does that one have a good pedigree?"

"Miss," said the owner, "if she could speak, she wouldn't talk to either one of us."

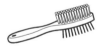

THE DIFFERENCE BETWEEN PET DOGS AND SHOW DOGS

PET DOGS SHED . . . . *Show dogs blow coat*

PET DOGS GO INTO HEAT . . . *Show dogs come into season*

PET DOGS RUN . . . . *Show dogs gait*

PET DOGS STAND . . . . *Show dogs stack*

PET DOGS GET A BATH . . . . *Show dogs are groomed*

PET DOGS BEG FOR TREATS . . . . *Show dogs desire bait*

PET DOGS RAID THE GARBAGE . . . .
. . . . *Show dogs show a natural tendency for scent articles*

PET DOGS POOP . . . . *Show dogs toilet*

AT THE HEIGHT OF THE COLD WAR, the Americans and Russians held a summit and decided to settle the arms race with one dogfight. Each side agreed to a five-year period during which they would each attempt to breed the best fighting dog in the world. The side that won would dominate the world, and the other would give up its weapons.

The Russians found the biggest, meanest Dobermans and Rottweilers in the world and bred them with the biggest, meanest Siberian wolves. They selected only the biggest and strongest puppy from each litter. They used steroids and trainers, and after five years came up with the biggest, meanest dog the world had ever seen. Its cage needed steel bars, and nobody could get near it without protective gloves and body armor.

When the day came for the dogfight, the Americans showed up with a nine-foot-long Dachshund. The Russians were

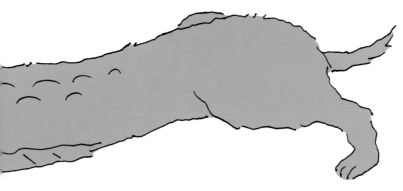

puzzled. It was obvious that this dog couldn't possibly last ten seconds with their dog. What were the Americans thinking?

When the cages were opened up, the Dachshund came out of its cage and waddled over toward the Russian dog. The Russian dog snarled and leaped out of its cage toward the dachshund. But, when it got close enough to bite the dachshund's neck, the dachshund opened its mouth and ate the Russian dog in one bite.

"How could this have happened?" exclaimed the Russian dog breeders. "We had our best people working for five years with the meanest Dobermans and Rottweilers in the world and the biggest, meanest Siberian wolves!"

"Well," replied the American breeders. "We had our best plastic surgeons working for five years to make an alligator look like a Dachshund."

When Breeds Collide

What do you get when you cross a…

Bloodhound and a Borzoi
A Bloody Bore

Pointer and an English Setter
A Poinsetter

Collie and a Lhasa Apso
A Collapso

Terrier and a Bulldog
A Terribull

Bloodhound and a Labrador
A BLABRADOR

Mutt and a Poodle
A MUDDLE

Newfoundland and a Basset Hound
NEWFOUND ASSET HOUND

Malamute and a Pointer
A MOOT POINT

Deer Hound and a Terrier
A DERRIERE

A DACHSHUND AND A BULLDOG had been great friends for years. The Bulldog was a real partier and loved to go out clubbing at night, but the Dachshund could never go: his owners expected him to stay home and guard the house at night. Eventually, the Bulldog came up with a plan: if the Dachshund made a puddle, his owners would put him out for the night, so he could sneak away and go out on the town.

The Dachshund gave it a try. The next evening the bulldog showed up, ready for a night out. He found the Dachshund moping on the front stoop.

"What's up?" he asked. "You don't look so happy for a dog who is about to get his groove on."

"It's not going to work," said the Dachshund gloomily. "I tried the puddle thing. They rubbed my nose in it."

"Oh, come on," said the Bulldog. "It's over soon enough, then you're free for the night."

"Easy for you to say with a nose like yours," said the Dachshund.

A FARMER wanted to take inventory of his sheep, so he asked his sheepdog to go to the field and count them.

The dog ran into the field, counted them, and ran back to his master.

"So," said the farmer, "how many do we have?"

"Forty," the dog replied.

"How can there be 40?" the farmer asked. "I only bought 38!"

"I know," said the dog. "But I rounded them up."

🐾

How many dogs does it take to put in a light bulb?

Golden Retriever
The sun is shining, the day is young, we've got our whole lives ahead of us, and you're inside worrying about a light bulb?

Border Collie
Just one. And I'll replace any wiring that's not up to code.

Dachshund
I can't reach the stupid lamp!

Toy Poodle
I'll just blow in the Border Collie's ear and he'll do it. By the time he finishes rewiring the house, my nails will be dry.

Rottweiler
Make me!

Shih tzu
Let the servants do it.

Lab
Oh, me, me!!! Pleeeeeeze let me change the light bulb! Can I? Can I? Huh? Huh? Can I?

MALAMUTE
Let the Border Collie do it. You can feed me while he's busy.

COCKER SPANIEL
Why change it? I can still pee on the carpet in the dark.

DOBERMAN PINSCHER
While it's dark, I'm going to sleep on the couch.

CHAPTER 5
DOG HAIKU

Meditations on Being a Dog

Why does she always reject my gifts?
I know she doesn't have
A dead squirrel already

Scraps of food
Rain down from the table
Like manna from heaven

I left a present
Well, not really a present
On your bedroom rug

My human is home!
Joy oozes from me
Onto the kitchen floor

The sound of my dog treats
Shaking inside their box
It's like the angels singing

Big interview today
I give my master good luck paw prints
On his new white shirt

My tail in my mouth
I form a perfect circle
That goes round and round

How do I love thee?
The ways are as infinite
As my hairs on the rug

She's late coming home again
My empty bowl
Mocks me

I feel it in my fur
The season of the fleas
Is upon us again

CHAPTER 6
SHAGGY DOG STORIES

Shaggy Dog Story n. 1. an extremely long-winded, tall tale,

2. an actual story about a shaggy dog, and

3. both of the above

IN FAR NORTHERN CANADA, there lived a trapper named DuLac. He was a poor man, but literate, and he shared his small home with several well-thumbed adventure novels and a large shaggy dog named Jacques.

Jacques didn't have much of a pedigree. He seemed to be a mix of terrier, wolfhound, and husky. But he was big and friendly and, fortunately for that very cold climate, had an exceptionally thick, shaggy coat.

One day, DuLac went to visit a fellow trapper, but his hut was empty. On the table was a newspaper. He eagerly read it from cover to cover. On the back page, an item caught his eye. Way down in the southern part of the province, there was an eccentric millionaire who was offering half his fortune to the person who could fulfill his dying wish—to own a really shaggy dog.

DuLac read the notice with great interest. At last, a way to make his fortune. No more bitter winters, loneliness, and hardship. He would set south with Jacques, make the dying millionaire happy, and in the process, set himself up for life. It would be a long journey in the cold of winter, but it would be worth it. Back home, he filled a backpack, put on his snowshoes, rigged a makeshift leash for Jacques, and headed south.

Man and dog covered the harshest of terrain—fording icy streams, pushing through blizzards, falling through cracks in the ice, and sleeping in snow caves.

At last they reached civilization. Everywhere they stopped people would say, "Goodness, that's a shaggy dog you have there!"

Finally they reached the millionaire's hometown and Du-Lac spied the mansion at the top of a steep hill. Footsore and exhausted, they reached the front door. Hopeful of the reward that was within his grasp, DuLac rang the doorbell with his weather-beaten hand. Minutes later, the door opened and a butler stood in the doorway.

"I've come about the shaggy dog story in this newspaper," said DuLac, and he handed Jacques' leash to the butler.

The butler silently walked off with the dog, crossed the marble foyer, and ascended an impressive circular staircase. DuLac waited patiently on the doorstep, dreaming of the luxury soon to be his. At last the butler reappeared. Solemnly, he handed back the dog.

"Not that shaggy," he said, and shut the door.

SHAGGY TWO

IN THE DAYS OF KING ARTHUR, there was a knight who was on his way to do a heroic deed. He had been out all day, traveling across the countryside, and had ridden his poor horse until she was exhausted and lame in one foot.

He knew he had to let the animal rest, but he was on a mission from the king and his honor depended upon completing it.

Up ahead on the road, he saw an inn. He could stop there, he thought, and trade in his horse for another one. Anyone would be honored to give his or her horse in the service of the king.

The knight thundered into the inn's stable yard on his lame steed. "I must have a horse!" he cried. "The life of the king depends upon it!"

The stable keeper shook his head sadly. "I'm sorry, brave Sire. I have no horses. They've all been taken in the service of the king."

"You must have something," said the knight in desperation. "A pony, a donkey, a mule . . . anything at all . . ."

"Nothing . . . unless . . .," the stable keeper stopped from a moment, then shook his head. "No, no, I couldn't."

The knight's eyes lit up. "Tell me!"

The stable keeper led the knight into the stable. Inside was a dog, but no ordinary dog. This dog was a giant, almost as large as the horse the knight was riding. But it was also the filthiest, shaggiest, smelliest, mangiest dog the knight had ever seen.

Swallowing, the knight said, "I'll take it. Where is the saddle?"

The stable keeper walked over to a saddle near the dog and started gasping for breath, holding the walls to keep himself upright. "I can't do it," he told the knight.

"You must give me the dog!" cried the knight. "Why can't you?"

The stable keeper said, "I just couldn't send a knight out on a dog like this." He turned and came back with a tiny, well-groomed poodle with a bow in her hair. "Here, take her instead!"

AN OLD MAN lived in a run-down shack on the outskirts of town. He had no family and only a few possessions: a table and chair, a bed, a bag of hand tools, and his hound dog, Mace. Mace and his master lived from one day to the next on the money the man made doing odd jobs for the towns-people. The dog was just a normal hound, with one exception: while most dogs like to chew on grass occasionally, Mace loved it. When the old man was in town, Mace would spend the day in the yard in front of the house, chewing away on the lawn.

One bright, sunny morning the old man said good-bye to his dog and headed into town to work. He had a plumbing repair job to do for the day, and the money earned would cover food for a week. Inside the house and ready to start, the old man reached into the bag for his wrench. To his surprise, it wasn't there. He dumped the contents of the bag on the floor, but still no wrench. Reality set in. Without a wrench he couldn't finish the job, and without the pay—no money for food! Un-happily, he told the lady who hired him what the situation was. Although sympathetic to his plight, she told him she's have to hire someone else.

Sorrowfully, the old man walked home, head bowed and

shoulders stooped. A journey that normally took 15 minutes seemed to last forever. But finally the old shack came into view, and there was Mace in the distance, munching away as usual on the lawn. When the dog saw his master, he came running, tail wagging, telling the old man how glad he was to see him. Kneeling beside the hound, the man began to pet him, and through tear-filled eyes told the dog that there would be no supper tonight and no food for tomorrow. What's more, without money to buy a new wrench, he had no idea what the future held. It was the lowest moment of his life.

Suddenly, he caught a glimpse of something shining in the grass. When he saw what it was, his despair turned to instant to joy! It was the wrench! He had dropped it on his way out that morning, and it would have been lost forever had Mace not been eating farther away from the house than he usually did! The old man grabbed the dog, gave him a hug that almost suffocated him, and ran into the house. Reaching for a stub of pencil and the only piece of paper he had, he wrote a moving tribute to his canine companion. It started like this: "A grazing Mace, how sweet the hound that saved a wrench for me."

CHAPTER 7
FETCHING FOLLIES

A dog on a mission—comedy ensues

A CLOWN TOOK HIS DOG TO THE VET.

"He's a little overweight," said the vet. "Try feeding him some of this special dog food and get him some exercise. Make sure he runs around a bit. Try playing a game of fetch with him, for example."

"I can't play fetch with my dog," said the clown.

"Why not?" the vet asked.

"Well, isn't it obvious?" the clown said.

"He can't throw."

TWO HUNTING BUDDIES were always trying to outdo each other. One day, one of them arrived for their annual hunting trip with a new dog. "You're not going to believe it when you see what this dog can do," the first one said. "I'd say he's the most amazing retriever in the world."

"We'll see about that," said the second one, and they went out into the marsh and set up their decoys.

Not long afterward, a flock of mallards flew overhead and the hunters succeeded in knocking down one of the birds. The new dog's owner commanded him to go fetch the duck, and he dove off the boat, but instead of swimming, he trotted across the surface of the water.

The owner beamed with pride when the dog returned with the duck in his mouth. "See, what'd I tell ya? The best retriever in the world. Have you ever seen anything like it? He walks on water!"

"Give me a break," said the second hunter defensively, "that dog can't even swim."

A MAN WAS SHOWING OFF his Labrador's hunting abilities to his friend. They went down to a lake and the man said to the dog, "How many ducks are out there, boy?"

The dog raced off to the lake, came back a couple of minutes later, and barked twice. Seconds later, two ducks floated into view.

"That was incredible," said the friend. "Can he do it again?"

"Sure," said the man, and he asked the dog once again, "how many ducks are out there, boy?"

The dog ran off again, came back, and barked four times. Four ducks flew past just moments later.

"I gotta have that dog," the friend said. "I'll give you 500 dollars and all of my hunting dogs." They agreed to the deal, and the second man took the dog home.

The next day, the man drove the dog and his wife down to the lake so he could show her their amazing new pet.

"How many ducks are out there, boy?" he asked the dog.

The dog ran off, came back, grabbed a stick, shook it, and tossed it over his shoulder.

The wife looked at her husband and rolled her eyes. "You mean to tell me you spent 500 dollars and gave away all our dogs for that?" she asked.

"But I saw him do it!" he replied. "Let me try again. How many ducks are out there, boy?"

The dog ran away again, came back, grabbed a stick, shook it, and tossed it over his shoulder. The wife just shook her head and went back to the house, and the man put the dog in the car and took him back to his original owner.

"I don't know how you did it, but you really got me good," he said. "This dog is useless. I tried doing exactly what you did and all the dog did was pick up a stick and wave it back and forth."

"You idiot," said the first owner. "He was trying to tell you there were more ducks than you could shake a stick at!"

A RABBI WAS MOVING OUT OF TOWN and had to give his young dog away. He gave it to one of his congregants, who was happy to take him.

Since the dog was scarcely more than a pup, the new owner had to train him. He started with the easiest commands, such as sit and stay, and found that the dog already knew a lot.

After a couple of weeks, he thought the dog was ready for something a little more difficult. He took him to the park, picked up a stick, and threw it, commanding the dog, "Fetch!"

The dog looked up at his master and started to whine, "Oy, the dog food you're feeding me. It's dreck, I tell you, compared to what I got at the rabbi's. And what about my dog bed? What, you can't wash it once in a while? It's covered in dirt. You think it's easy being a dog? Wagging my tail all the time? It gives me such pain, you should only know . . ."

The man stared at his dog in astonishment, thought for a moment, and then thumped his head with an "I-get-it-now" gesture. "No, no, " he said, "I said fetch, not kvetch!"

CHAPTER 8
DOGS GONE POSTAL

The postman doesn't ring twice. He doesn't even make it to the doorstep.

A MAN'S GREAT DANE had a sweet disposition—with one exception: she went crazy when she saw the UPS truck come, and she'd invariably go after its driver. One day the man was returning from a walk with the dog when he ran into the UPS driver coming back to his truck after making a delivery. As usual, the dog went nuts. The owner pulled back on the leash and tried to get the dog under control. Flustered and embarrassed, he apologized to the driver. "As you can see, she loves UPS drivers," he said.

"Don't you feed her anything else?" the driver asked.

AN ANGRY MAIL CARRIER stormed into the post office after his daily rounds. Sensing he was upset, the supervisor asked him if there was something the matter.

Pointing to his torn and bloody pants leg, he explained how he had been repeatedly bitten by a German Shepherd on his route.

"Well, did you put anything on it?" the supervisor asked.

"No," the carrier replied. "The dog seemed to like it just fine plain."

A POSTMAN ARRIVED AT A HOUSE surrounded by a wire fence that held back two fierce-looking Dobermans. Close to the house, there was a man trimming the hedges.

"Excuse me," he called to the man. "Do your dogs bite?"

"No," the man said, shaking his head.

The postman opened the gate and entered the yard. The dogs lunged toward him and he just made it back out of the gate in time to escape their snapping jaws.

"I thought you said your dogs don't bite," the postman shouted angrily to the man at the hedges.

"Oh, I'm just the gardener here," he replied. "Those aren't my dogs."

A MAIL CARRIER was working his first day on a new route. He was a little nervous because the last carrier who had had the route had suddenly quit. Everything had been relatively uneventful until he came to a fence with a sign that read:

BEWARE OF PARROT!

He looked up on the front porch of the house and, sure enough, there was an innocent-looking parrot swinging on a perch. Nothing to worry about, he assured himself, just the homeowners making a joke. He opened the gate, walked up the front steps, and looked at the parrot with just a hint of trepidation. The parrot looked back at him and shifted a little on his perch.

The mailman chuckled to himself about the vicious attack parrot. He put the mail in the mailbox and started down the stairs. At the bottom of the steps sat a large, mean-looking Pit Bull. From behind him he heard the parrot squawk,

"Get him, Rex. Get him, Rex!"

A WOMAN HAD A DOG SHE JUST LOVED, but the dog had the bad habit of attacking visitors, especially the mail carrier. She took him to the vet, who suggested that if she neutered him, he'd probably quit his aggressive behavior. She went ahead with the operation.

A few days later, as she was sitting on her porch with the dog, the mail carrier arrived. The dog jumped up and went after her, knocking her to the ground.

The woman grabbed her dog and got him under control. "I'm so sorry," she said. "I just don't know what to do. The vet said that if I had him neutered he would get over his aggression."

"You should have had his teeth removed instead," the mail carrier said, brushing herself off. "I could tell he wasn't looking for sex when he came after me."

CHAPTER 9
PUPPY LOVE

Cute and cuddly canine comedy

TWO PUPPIES MEET EACH OTHER IN THE PARK. The first one says,

"Hi, I'M Fido. What's your name?"

"I don't know," says the second pup, **"But I think it's Down Boy."**

Q. WHAT'S THE DIFFERENCE BETWEEN A TEENAGER AND A PUPPY?

A BREEDER SOLD A LITTER OF PUPPIES from a pair of dogs who were both prizewinners. They were so sought after that she had buyers from around the world. She sold one puppy to a man in Egypt, who named the dog Ahmal. She sold another to a family in Mexico, who named the dog Juan. As the months went by, she found she really missed the puppies. She asked the family in Mexico if they would send a picture of their dog, and they did.

"He's so adorable," the woman sighed to her husband. "I wish I had a picture of Ahmal."

"What's the big deal," her husband said. "You've seen Juan, you've seen Ahmal."

ONE DAY A WOMAN WENT FOR A WALK in her neighborhood and came across a boy with some puppies. "Would you like a puppy?" he asked her. "They aren't ready for new homes quite yet, but they will be in a few weeks!"

"Oh, they're adorable," the lady exclaimed. "What kind of dogs are they?"

"These are optimists," said the little boy.

"That's nice," said the woman, thinking the little boy had confused the word with the name of a dog breed. "I'll ask my husband if he's interested in getting one."

She went home and told her husband. He was interested and went to see the puppies about a week later.

"Hey, mister, want a puppy?" the boy said as he approached.

"I think my wife spoke with you last week," the man said. "What kind of dogs are these?"

"They're pessimists," the boy said.

"Oh, I thought you told my wife they were optimists," the man said.

"Yeah, but they've opened their eyes since then," the boy explained.

How to Photograph a Puppy

1. Remove film from box and load camera.

2. Remove film box from puppy's month and throw in trash.

3. Remove puppy from trash and brush coffee grounds from his nose.

4. Choose a suitable background for photo.

5. Mount camera on tripod and focus.

6. Remove dirty sock from puppy's mouth.

7. Place puppy in spot and return to camera.

8. Forget about spot and crawl after puppy on knees.

9. Focus camera with one hand and fend off puppy with other hand.

10. Get tissue and clean nose print from lens.

11. Put cat outside and put peroxide on the scratch on puppy's nose.

12. Put magazines back on coffee table.

13. Try to get puppy's attention by squeaking toy over your head.

14. Replace your glasses and check camera for damage.

15. Jump up in time to grab puppy by scruff of neck and say, "No, outside! No, outside!!"

16. Call spouse to clean up mess.

17. Fix a drink.

18. Sit back in recliner with drink and resolve to teach puppy "sit" and "stay" first thing in the morning.

CHAPTER 10
ASSORTED TREATS

A little of this and that

A BANKER'S DOG, a criminal's dog, and a high school student's dog were gathered outside the local meat market looking at a side of beef in the window. They were discussing ways to get their paws on it.

"Why don't we go in and offer to pay for the side of beef on an installment plan," said the banker's dog. "Interest rates are low right now, and I know I can get us a good deal."

"No, that would take too long..." said the criminal's dog. "Why don't we just run in there? You distract him and I'll grab it and run."

"I have a better idea," the student's dog said. "Why don't we sit out here and whine . . . they'll just give it to us."

A POLICE OFFICER and his K-9 partner were sitting in a parked police van on the side of the road. A little boy looked in the back of the van, then came around to the officer's window and knocked.

The officer rolled down the window.

"Is that a dog you've got back there?" the boy asked.

"It sure is," the policeman replied.

The boy looked back at the van, then back to the officer. "What'd he do?" asked the boy.

DURING BREAK TIME at obedience school, two dogs were talking. "The thing I hate about obedience school," one said, "is that you learn all this stuff that you'll never use in the real world."

A COUPLE OF SKIERS get caught in an avalanche. They are about to panic, when suddenly, across the drifts of snow, they see a St. Bernard coming with a barrel of rum around his neck.

"Look!" says one. "It's man's best friend!"

"Yes," says the second. "And it's being carried by a dog!"

TWO CITY SLICKERS thought they'd give duck hunting a try. They got a license, bought a dog, and set out to a hunting retreat.

After spending about four hours in the blind, the first guy complained.

"We spent all this money on the license and dog, and we haven't got even one duck."

"I told you," said the second guy. "You aren't throwing the dog high enough!"

TWO DOGS were watching some dancers doing some fancy moves at a nightclub.

"Have you ever tried that?" the first dog asked.

"Only once," the second dog said. "As soon as I started to dance, my owner picked me up, rushed me to the vet, and the crazy doc pumped me full of worm pills."

WHILE DRIVING DOWN a lonely stretch of country road, a man came upon a young guy running very hard with three Dobermans snarling at his heels. The man screeched his car to a halt and threw open the door.

"Get in, get in!" he shouted.

"Thanks," puffed the guy as he opened the door. "I really appreciate it. Most people won't stop when they see I have three dogs!"

AN OLD WOMAN WAS CLEANING HER ATTIC with her faithful dog by her side. Among the boxes she found a little oil lamp. She picked it up, and just for fun, rubbed it a little with a dust rag. To her shock, a puff of smoke arose from it, and a genie appeared.

"Hello, my mistress," the genie said. "I am here to grant you three wishes."

The woman thought for a moment and said, "I wish I was the most beautiful young woman in the world."

The genie nodded and a puff of smoke surrounded her. When it dissolved, the genie handed her a mirror. Sure enough, she was beautiful.

"I wish I had more money than I knew what to do with," she said.

Once more the smoke appeared, and when it dissolved, a duffle bag of cash lay in front of her.

"I wish you would turn Spot here into a gorgeous young man," the woman announced.

Smoke surrounded her dog and when it cleared, in his place was a handsome young man with chiseled features and a body to die for.

She walked over to him. He put his arms around her, brushed his hand upon her cheek, and murmured, "Now, aren't you sorry you had me neutered?"

A TALENT SCOUT IS WALKING DOWN THE STREET when he hears someone singing in an amazing voice. He follows the sound of the voice around the corner until he finds a man and a young dog sitting in an alleyway. The dog is the one singing. He finishes the song and the agent claps. "Excuse me, sir," the agent says to the dog's owner. "I'm a talent scout and I know talent when I hear it. This dog could be a real star. I could get him a recording contract in no time. I'd love to represent you, if you'll just come back with me to my office around the corner."

The man agrees and they all head back to the office. While the agent is preparing the papers, the dog sings a few more numbers just to show his range. He's in the middle of a soulful rendition of "My Girl" when the door opens and a large dog comes in, grabs him by the scruff of the neck, and carries him away.

"Wait! Come back!" cries the agent. "That pup can make us all rich!"

"It's no use," replies the dog's owner. "That's his mother. She wants him to be a doctor."